Playing in Keys for Cello

Book One:

C, G, and F major

by Cassia Harvey

CHP242

©2013 by C. Harvey Publications All Rights Reserved.
6403 N. 6th Street
Philadelphia, PA 19126
www.charveypublications.com

Playing in C Major

Cassia Harvey

A key is like a language: every key contains certain notes and has certain rules.

The key of C major contains all the natural notes on the cello.

There are no sharps or flats in C major.

The notes in the key of C major are all of the notes in the C major scale,
so we will start by learning the notes in the C major scale that occur in first position.

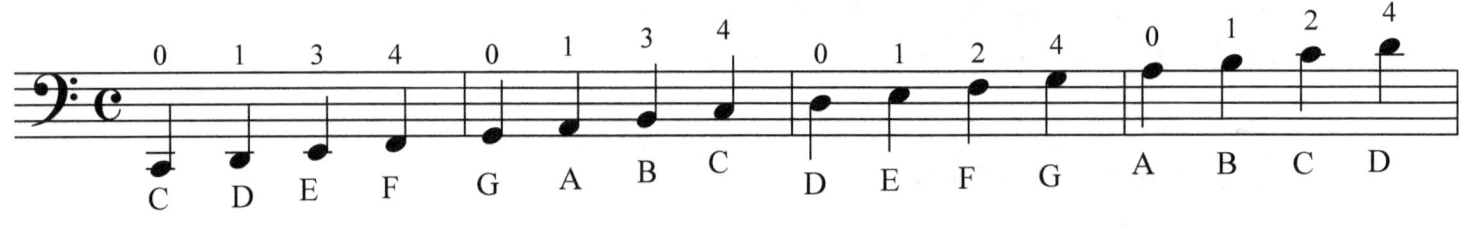

On the cello, the key of C major uses
2nd finger on the A and D strings and
3rd finger on the G and C strings: "2, 2, 3, 3".

©2013 C. Harvey Publications All Rights Reserved.

St. Paul's Steeple

Trad., arr. Harvey

The Woman and the Peddler

Trad., arr. Harvey

C Major Study No. 1

C Major Scale Patterns

A Song Tune

Purcell, arr. Harvey

March in C

Purcell, arr. Harvey

C Major Study No. 2

C Major Study No. 3

©2013 C. Harvey Publications All Rights Reserved.

C Major Study No. 4

Gavotta

Purcell, arr. Harvey

Vivace from Violin Concerto

Telemann, arr. Harvey

C Major Patterns

Playing in Keys for Cello, Book One

C Major Study No. 5

Arlequin Marie Sa Fille

Trad., arr. Harvey

The Little Sparrow

Trad., arr. Harvey

Arpeggio and Broken Thirds

2nd and 3rd Fingers Across Strings

Devil's Dream

Trad., arr. Harvey

Pray Goody

Trad., arr. Harvey

G Major Scale

G Major Notes on G, D, and A

2nd and 3rd Fingers in G Major

G Major Finger Patterns

Playing in Keys for Cello, Book One

March

Handel, arr. Harvey

©2013 C. Harvey Publications All Rights Reserved.

G Major Study No. 1

Playing in Keys for Cello, Book One

March from Pietro L'Eremita

Rossini, arr. Harvey

Hornpipe

Trad., arr. Harvey

Playing in Keys for Cello, Book One

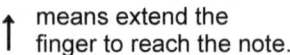
means extend the finger to reach the note.

Stretching to E to Reach F#

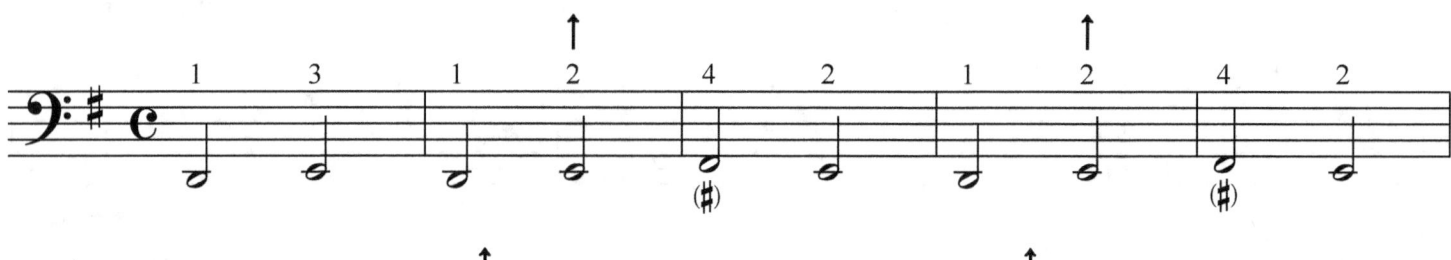

Stretching for F#

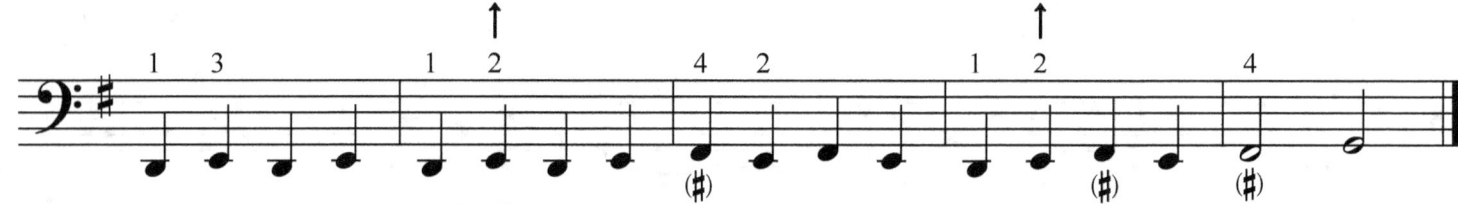

Stretching in Scale Patterns

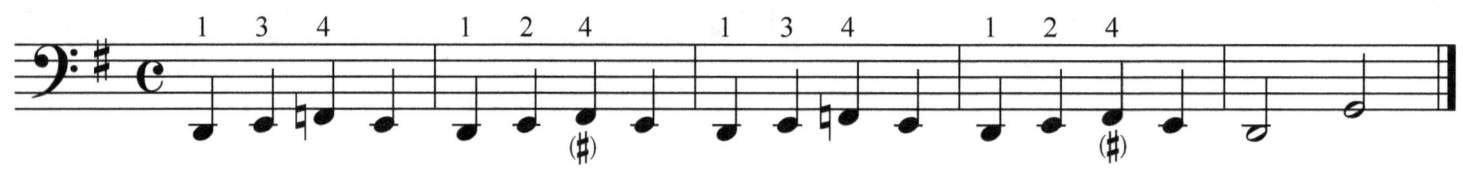

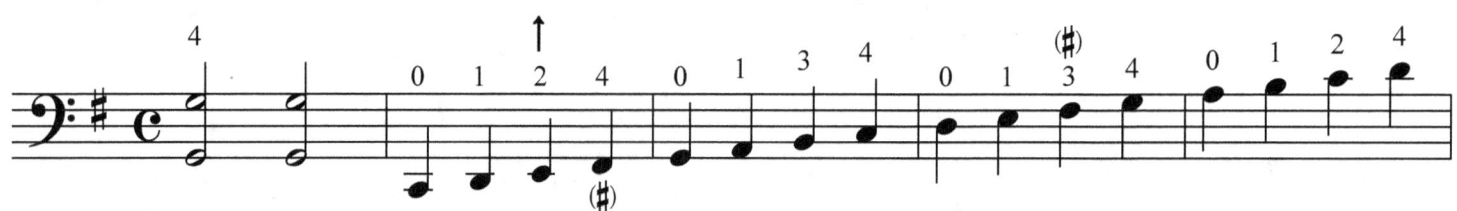

Stretching Across Strings

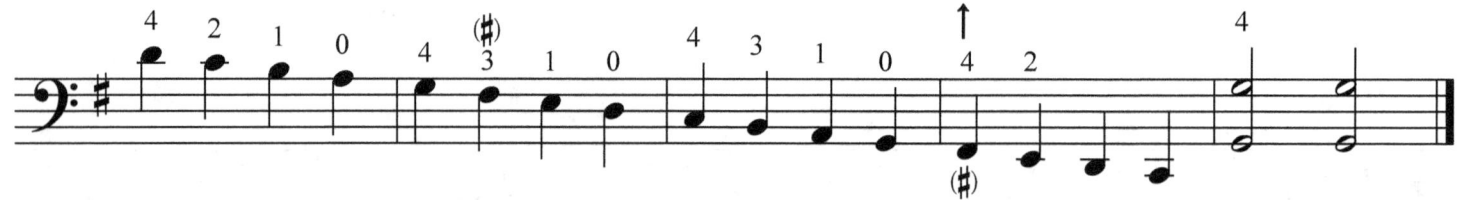

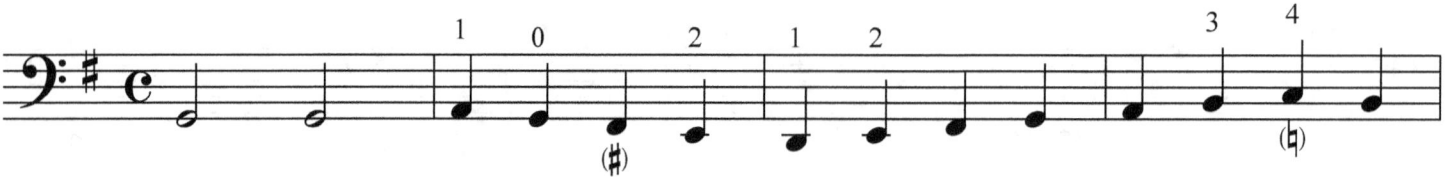

©2013 C. Harvey Publications All Rights Reserved.

French Melody

Fra Tanta Angoscie

Caraffa, arr. Harvey

Stretching Exercise No. 1

Stretching Across Strings

Berlin Waltz

Trad., arr. Harvey

The Market Chorus

Auber, arr. Harvey

Stretching Exercise No. 2

Stretching Exercise No. 3

Playing in Keys for Cello, Book One

Quick Step

Trad., arr. Harvey

F Major Scale

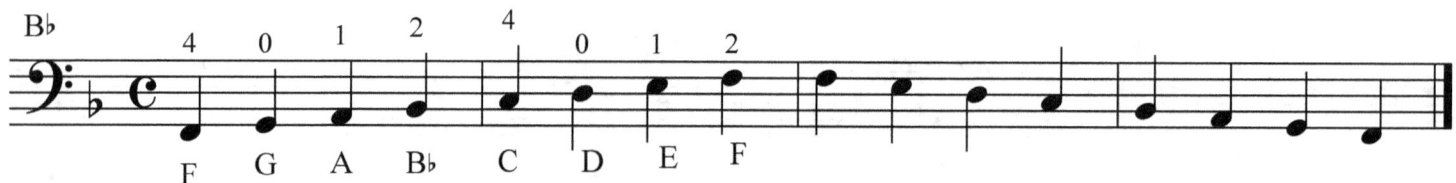

F Major Across Strings

F Major Finger Patterns

F Major Study No. 1

Allegretto
Kling, arr. Harvey

Contredanse
Bast, arr. Harvey

F Major Patterns Across Strings

F Major Study No. 2

Glasgow Quadrille

Trad., arr. Harvey

E's and F's

Octaves and Other Intervals

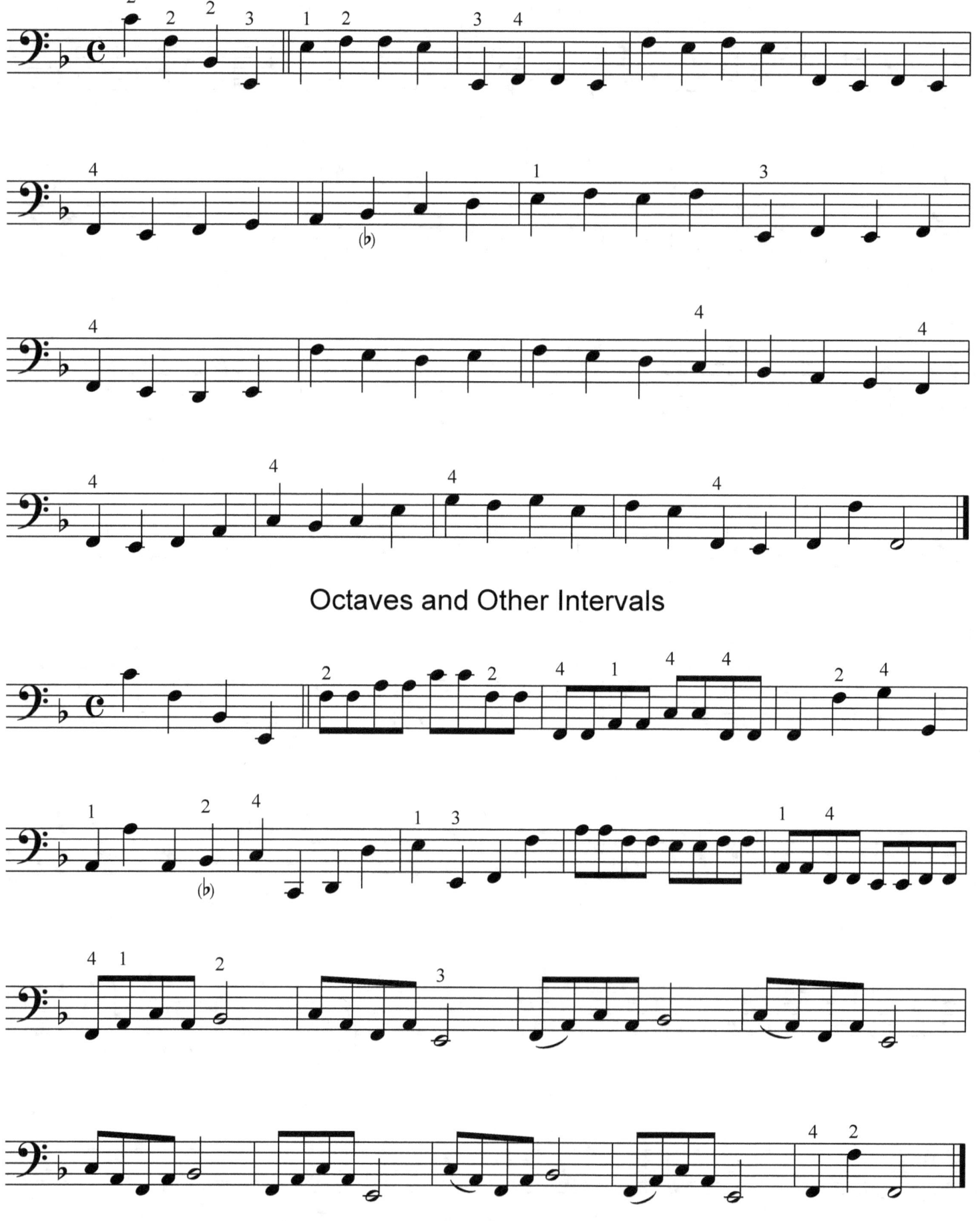

Playing in Keys for Cello, Book One

The Portreath Hornpipe

Bain, arr. Harvey

The Yellow-Haired Laddie

Trad., arr. Harvey

E♮ and B♭ Across Strings

F Major Study No. 2

Playing in Keys for Cello, Book One 41

The Fairy Dance Reel
Trad., arr. Harvey

The Devil Among the Tailors
Trad., arr. Harvey

©2013 C. Harvey Publications All Rights Reserved.

Stretching Back to B♭

More Stretching

Playing in Keys for Cello, Book One

Over the Rolling Hills
Harvey

Rigaudon
Rameau, arr. Harvey

©2013 C. Harvey Publications All Rights Reserved.

Reaching B♭ from Open A

Across Strings and Stretching

Cavatine from the Marriage of Figaro

Mozart, arr. Harvey

Overture to "The Deserter"

Monsigny, arr. Harvey

Stretching in Slurs

F Major Study No. 3

A Stately Minuet
Harvey

Sonatina
Beethoven, arr. Harvey

Intervals

F Major Study No. 4

©2013 C. Harvey Publications All Rights Reserved.

Hornpipe

Aldridge, arr. Harvey

Valse de Paris

Trad., arr. Harvey

Switching Keys:
Really think; this is harder than it looks!

Playing in Keys for Cello, Book One — 51

The Downfall of Paris, in C Major

Trad., arr. Harvey

©2013 C. Harvey Publications All Rights Reserved.

The Downfall of Paris, in G Major

Playing in Keys for Cello, Book One

Trad., arr. Harvey

©2013 C. Harvey Publications All Rights Reserved.

Playing in Keys for Cello, Book One

The Downfall of Paris, in F Major

Trad., arr. Harvey

©2013 C. Harvey Publications All Rights Reserved.

Playing in Keys for Cello, Book One

Song, in C Major

Parsons, arr. Harvey

Song, in G Major

Song, in F Major

©2013 C. Harvey Publications All Rights Reserved.

available from www.charveypublications.com: CHP272

Flying Fiddle Duets for Two Cellos, Book One

John Ryan's Polka

Trad., arr. Myanna Harvey

©2015 C. Harvey Publications. All Rights Reserved.

www.ingramcontent.com/pod-product-compliance
Lightning Source LLC
Chambersburg PA
CBHW051424070526
44584CB00023B/3570